WILLIAM GELL'S TOUR IN THE LAKES

William Gell *(1830) by T Uwins. (By courtesy of the National Portrait Gallery, London.)*

A TOUR IN THE LAKES
1797
by
William Gell

edited and introduced by
William Rollinson

with an afterword by
Melvyn Bragg

SMITH SETTLE

First published in 2000 by
Smith Settle Ltd
Ilkley Road
Otley
West Yorkshire
LS21 3JP

ISBN 1 85825 139 7

Set in Monotype Bulmer.

Designed, printed and bound by
SMITH SETTLE
Ilkley Road, Otley, West Yorkshire LS21 3JP

Introduction

The Lakers

It is no exaggeration to say that the English Lake District was 'discovered' in the eighteenth century. This was a century of enlightenment, an age of curiosity, and this is reflected in the writings of the early tourists to the Lake District.

Two major factors were influential in opening up the Lakes to tourists. The first was the general improvement in travelling and road conditions in the eighteenth century, largely resulting from the development of turnpikes. Although travelling by road was still something of an adventure, it had lost most of the dangers with which it had once been associated.

The second factor which contributed to the discovery of the Cumbrian mountains was the European political situation; the unrest and bloodshed on the Continent meant that the 'Grand Tour', that most important part of an English gentleman's education, was at best difficult if not impossible, and consequently attention was turned to the hitherto unexplored parts of Britain, to Snowdonia, Derbyshire, the Highlands of Scotland, and the Lake District.

Of course, the Lakes had been visited by 'off-comers' since the sixteenth century — John Leland and William Camdem passed through Cumbria in their search for antiquities, Celia Fiennes in 1689 undertook her 'Great Journey to Newcastle and to Cornwall' and recorded a lucid but brief account of her stay — but these were visits lasting at the most a few days and were usually made during the course of a much longer tour. However, the eighteenth century marked the beginning of the Romantic movement, and in particular the advent of 'the Lakers ... those persons who visit the beautiful scenes in Cumberland and Westmorland by distinction called the Lakes.'[1]

The poet Thomas Gray was one of the first genuine 'Lakers', and the account of his tour in 1769[2] set the pattern for those who followed in his footsteps. Gray's attitude was one of respectful awe: he expected to be shocked by the Cumbrian hills and mountains, and he was not disappointed. But Gray, like most of his contemporaries, was a timid soul as far as mountains were concerned; he was quite content to view their 'horrible grandeur' and 'rude and terrible magnificence' from the safety of the valley floor. Even the sight of Gowdar Crag reminded him of

1. *European Magazine*, volume 34, 1798, quoted in Nicholson, N, *The Lakers*, 1955.

2. Gray, T, *Journal in the Lakes*, 1775.

places in the Alps, ' … where the guides tell you to move with speed, and say nothing, lest the agitation of the air should loosen the snows above, and bring down a mass that would overwhelm a caravan'.

Yet Gray's picture of 'Beauty in the lap of Horror' excited general curiosity and attracted other travellers to the area. In 1772, William Gilpin made his tour, subsequently publishing his observations in 1786,[3] and in 1778 the Jesuit priest Father Thomas West produced the first and most popular guidebook, so setting the fashion for 'scenic tourism'. The work attempted to conduct the genteel tourist in search of the Picturesque to the classic viewpoints or 'stations', where the vista was described in meticulous detail. So popular was West's *Guide to the Lakes* that ten editions were published by 1812.[4] In 1783, Peter Crosthwaite, self-styled 'Admiral of the Keswick Regatta, Keeper of the Museum at Keswick, Pilot, Geographer and Hydrographer to the Nobility and Gentry', began to issue a series of maps of the major lakes on which he indicated West's 'stations'[5] in an attempt to assist the 'Lakers' in their search for the Picturesque.

However, by this time much of the excitement had been

3. Gilpin, W, *Observations Relative Chiefly to Picturesque Beauty made in the year 1772, in several parts of England, particularly in the Mountains and Lakes of Cumberland and Westmorland*, 1786.

4. Bicknell, P, *The Picturesque Scenery of the Lake District*, 1990.

5. Crosthwaite, P, *A Series of Accurate Maps of the Principal Lakes of Cumberland, Westmorland and Lancashire*, facsimile edition, 1968, with an introduction and notes by William Rollinson.

6. Nicolson, N, *op cit.*

taken out of a tour to the Lakes — indeed, the excursion became more of a fashion than an adventure. Norman Nicholson has suggested that, by the late eighteenth century, ' … the Picturesque was already becoming a planned pleasure, a Butlin Camp of the sensibilities with all its possibilities tasted, tested, tried, recorded, and all mapped out.'[6] It is to this period that the William Gell tour belongs, for it is an account of an excursion made during a long vacation from Cambridge, a trip which included visits to the Bowder Stone, Lyulph's Tower, Lodore Falls, Scale Force, Pocklington's Island in Derwentwater and all the other 'recognised' sights which became an accepted part of a 'Laker's' itinerary.

The Manuscript

The manuscript was purchased by the Barrow-in-Furness Public Library in 1951 for thirty shillings (£1.50). It consists of sixty-four closely-written pages and some forty pages of watercolours, pencil sketches, and maps of the lakes copied from Crosthwaite's surveys. There are several blank pages and the remains of pages which have been torn out of the book. Many of the sketches and

The first page from William Gell's manuscript.

paintings are unfinished. The whole is bound in boards and measures five and a half inches by nine inches; the paper is hand-made and bears the Whatman watermark, but is undated. The handwriting is very legible, and there is evidence that large parts of the manuscript were written in pencil before being re-written in ink. In two places an attempt has been made to obliterate the handwriting by superimposing black watercolour paint or ink, but most of what was written may be read with the aid of ultra-violet light.

The front cover bears the inscription in pencil 'Sir William Gell' and 'Sir Buswick Harwood', and from evidence contained in the manuscript it seems that it was written by Gell, though Harwood may have made the pencilled comments which occur within the text in a hand which is certainly not that of the principal author. A comparison of the handwriting in the manuscript with a specimen of Sir William's hand in letters to Lord Hardwicke[7], now in the British Library, reinforces this view.

Although the manuscript has no date, it is possible to assign it to the year 1797 on the basis of two pieces of evidence: first, the author occasionally gives the date and

7. BM Additional Ms 35,652.

the day of the month, for example Sunday the 2nd July and Tuesday the 4th July, combinations which occurred in that year; and secondly, referring to Pocklington's Island in Derwentwater, he remarks that Pocklington 'has just sold this spot to Mr. Peachy'. The date of the sale, 1796, is recorded by Peter Crosthwaite on his map of the island.[8]

Although the manuscript is not signed in his own hand by William Gell, there can be no doubt that he was the author. But what of his companions? He refers to 'the doctor', and from the pencilled name 'Sir Buswick Harwood' on the front cover, it seems possible that 'the doctor' and 'Sir Buswick' are one and the same person. Harwood was a colourful Cambridge academic; elected to the Chair of Anatomy in 1785, he spent most of his academic life studying transfusion of the blood. In 1800 he was appointed Downing Professor of Medicine in the university, and was knighted six years later. He died in Downing College in 1814 aged about sixty-nine.

Of the other members of the party, little is known. By chance, another Cambridge academic, James Plumptre (1770–1832), was visiting the Lakes at the same time as Gell's party.[9] His journal confirms that he '... had breakfast

8. Crosthwaite, P, *op cit.*

9. Quoted in Bicknell, P, and Woof, R, *The Discovery of the Lake District, 1750-1810*, 1982.

with Messrs Gell, Skrine, Hornsly and Chatfield' in Grasmere. Skrine was probably Henry Skrine (1755-1803), the
topographer; were he and the others part of William Gell's
party?

The Author

William Gell was born at Hopton, near Wirksworth,
Derbyshire, in 1777, the son of Philip Gell and his wife,
Dorothy Milnes.[10] Educated at Jesus College, Cambridge,
William later became a Fellow of Emmanuel College. He
graduated Bachelor of Arts in 1798 and took the degree of
Master of Arts in 1804, having been elected Fellow of the
Society of Antiquaries the previous year. From then on
his academic reputation was meteoric: he was made a
member of the society of Dilettanti and a Fellow of the
Royal Society in 1807.

He travelled widely in Italy, Greece and Asia Minor,
and as a result he wrote several books on the history and
topography of these regions, including one of the earliest
accounts of the excavations at Pompeii. Many of his published works are illustrated with sketches made in the
field, for at one time he was trained in the schools of the

10. Clay, Edith, *Sir William Gell in Italy,* 1976.

Royal Academy, though there is no evidence that he exhib-
ited. His paintings 'have been praised for their exactness
and minuteness, though they do not show any exceptional
power'[11], a statement which is perhaps borne out by the
illustrations which accompany the manuscript tour of the
Lakes, though it must be remembered that this was produced when he was an undergraduate and before he received artistic training.

11. *Dictionary of National Biography.*

His reputation as a topographer was widely known.
Byron in *English Bards* referred to Gell in the well-known
couplet:

Of Dardan tours, let dilettanti tell,

I leave topography to classic Gell

Byron had originally written 'coxcomb' in his manuscript,
but altered the word to more charitable 'classic' before
publication. In the fifth edition of this work he changed
his mind yet again, and altered 'classic' to 'rapid' with a
note 'rapid indeed!'.[12]

12. Clay, Edith, *op cit.*

Gell's eye for landscape inevitably led him to carto-
graphy, a field in which he excelled. His 1834 map of *The
Topography of* Rome *and its Environs* is a masterpiece
which took him at least five years to survey and engrave

13. Frederiksen, M, in Clay, Edith, *op cit.*

14. The obituary in *The Gentleman's Magazine* (1836) and the *Dictionary of National Biography* give 1803 as the date of the knighthood. This is incorrect. I am indebted to Mr. M R Bruce for this information.

and which has been described as 'a testimony to strong convictions'.[13]

William Gell was knighted by the Prince Regent at Carlton House in May 1814.[14] It must have been somewhat galling to the prince when, three months later, Sir William joined the intimate circle which surrounded the estranged Princess Caroline of Wales, and he travelled extensively with her court in Italy and the Middle East. He later gave evidence at her trial in 1820, where he stoutly defended her honour.

By all accounts, Gell was a most amusing companion, both witty and entertaining, as well as an accomplished guitarist. Inordinately fond of dogs, it is said that he even taught one to sing.

After 1820 Sir William spent most of his time at his villa in Naples. Incapacitated by rheumatism and gout, he had to be carried about in a chair. He died on the 4th February 1836, and is buried in the Protestant cemetery in Naples.

William Gell and the Wordsworths

William Gell was clearly impressed by the scenery of the Lake District to such an extent that, either in 1798 or 1799, he built a cottage on the western shores of Grasmere.

James Plumptre, who had met Gell in Grasmere in 1797 (see page xi), decided to call on his fellow Cambridge graduate in July, 1799. He records in his journal:

> Walked to Grassmere to call upon Gell and see his new house. He has bought about ½ an acre of ground, part of it rock and on that he has built a small house only one story high with two small sitting rooms, in one of which is an organ, two very small bedrooms and a small Kitchen. There are a few old trees about it, and it commands a beautiful view of the Lake. Gell not at home.[15]

15. Quoted in Bicknell, P, and Woof, R, *op cit.*

In late December 1799, William Wordsworth and his sister, Dorothy, moved into Dove Cottage on the outskirts of Grasmere, and it was inevitable that the Wordsworths and Gell should meet. Although the extent of their friendship is not clear, they were certainly on amicable terms, and the Wordsworths had permission to use William Gell's boat on the lake. On several occasions Dorothy records in her journal such entries as:

> *16th May 1800:* ... walked to Mr. Gells with the Books, gathered mosses and plants.
> *29th May 1800:* ... went to Mr. Gell's boat before tea.

'Mr Gell's cottage, Grasmere',
a watercolour by Christine Denmead
after J Harden.

9th June 1800: we went to R. Newton's for pike-
floats and went round to Mr. Gell's Boat and on
to the Lake to fish.

13th June 1800: Mr. Gell and his party came.

24 November, 1801: We could not get into Mr.
Gell's grounds — the old tree fallen from its
undue exaltation above the Gate.

The final reference to Gell in the journal occurs on the
6th May 1802 when Dorothy records that:

The ladies are come to Mr. Gell's cottage. We
saw them as we went and their light when we
returned.

But it is perhaps not surprising that contact ceased,
since in 1803 William Gell was sent on a diplomatic mission
to the Ionian Islands, from 1804 to 1806 he was travelling
widely in Greece and the islands, and thereafter was caught
up in the hectic round of travel, writing, the London
social scene and, later, court life as part of the entourage of
Princess Caroline. Did he ever again find time to visit his
beloved Lake District and renew his acquaintance with
the Wordsworths?

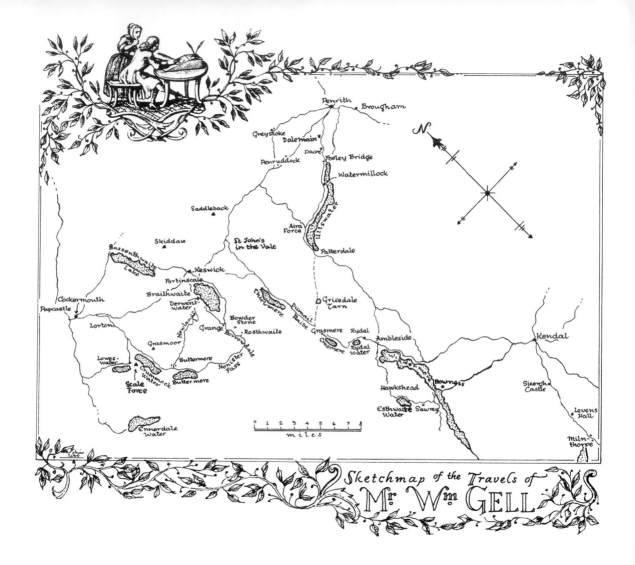

Sketchmap of the Travels of Mr. Wm. GELL

A Journal of a Tour in the Lakes made in 1797 by William Gell

Editor's note: the spelling and punctuation of the original manuscript have been retained.

We [the doctor[1] and myself] set out on the ninteenth of June from Kendal in Westmorland to join the rest of our party who had arrived some days before us at Grassmere and had procured a convenient lodging there both for themselves and us. From Kendal to Grassmere is a stage of eighteen miles and though the first part of the way has nothing in it to attract attention or render it agreeable yet the recollection of it soon ceases on the unexpected sight

1. Probably Buswick Harwood.

View looking down Windermere by Joseph Farington. '… the unexpected sight of Windermere from the summit of an hill over which the road lies'.

Low Wood Inn, with Windermere and the Langdale Pikes in the background, by Ackermann. '... Low wood an inn within forty yards of the lake and two miles from Ambleside'.

of Windermere from the summit of an hill over which the road lies.

At first the lake assumed the appearance of a noble river, in one part almost covered with Islands full of trees or shrubs down to the waters edge, but on a nearer approach the breadth encreased and the lake acquires a majesty which the apparent narrowness had before denied it. The road passes about 4 miles along the water side through the villages of Bowness and Rayrigg to Calgarth and Low

wood an inn within forty yards of the lake and two miles from Ambleside. We passed through Ambleside by Rydal Hall and water till at a turn of the road we perceived the beautiful vale of Grassmere beneath us. Here we found

Rydal Hall from Fox Howe, an 1832 engraving by G Pickering. 'We passed through Ambleside by Rydal Hall ...'

our Companions on their return from a neighbouring Tarn where they had fished all the morning. I myself was so impatient to try my success on the trout, that I could not wait till dinner was over before I took one with my line. During the first week we visited Rydal hall, and water and two cascades. The hall is the seat of Sir Michael le Flemming, a gentleman of a very hospitable disposition, and descended from one of the most ancient families in the Kingdom.[2] They had formerly large posessions in the Lordship[3] of Furness. The Hall on Coniston Water was the chief seat for many years but on a marriage with the heiress of Knott of Rydal they removed as I take it, and have since remained there. The house appears handsome and spacious, a little to the left from it, the shrubbery lies, under which is concealed the lower cascade, and is so artfully contrived as to make what is really nothing in itself at least pleasing if not grand.

We passed along a short winding path, closely bordered with young spruce or Silver firs, till we came to the door of a little low summer house, which on opening, presented us through a large square window in the opposite wall with a miniature of as beautiful and romantic a fall of water

2. The le Flemings were one of the most ancient and respected families in Cumbria. In the twelfth century they had received from Henry I certain lands in the Furness peninsula, but in the middle of the thirteenth century a branch of the family moved first to Coniston and later to Rydal.

3. The word 'Lordship' is written in pencil, for the author was clearly not sure of his facts. The le Flemings owned the manor of Muchland in Low Furness, a name derived from 'Michael's Land,' Michael le Fleming being the first owner.

An engraving of Lower Rydal Fall by Farington. '… as beautiful and romantic a fall of water as the imagination can conceive…'

as the imagination can conceive, within so very limited a compass. The rocks on each side are covered with moss, or those plants which are usually found in moist situations, trees hang over them, and in the center, the little stream pours itself through a narrow channel into a small bason not more than ten yards in diameter. The fall may be about twelve feet, a bridge some yards higher up the stream has a picturesque effect. The higher cascade though its fall be greater, yet fails in those beauties in which the lower excels, though much more retired than the other it wants the accompaniments of trees and gloom to render it so

4. Nothing pleased the early tourists more than cascades and waterfalls, the diaries and guidebooks of the period containing descriptions, accounts and measurements of all the major falls. Southey, when poet laureate, sang the praises of one of the most famous, Lodore, and Mr Pocklington, in his usual eccentric fashion, diverted the waters of Barrow Cascade in order to 'improve' the fall. On this occasion, William Gell's party visited Stockghyll Force near Ambleside, where they were clearly more impressed than they had been at Rydal. Gell estimated the fall to be thirty yards, but later on reflection he altered this to seventy feet.

5. An intriguing note in pencil records that 'here nero made an elegant fall down the cascade.' *Nero* is the modern Greek word for 'water'. Perhaps this is an instance of William Gell demonstrating his erudition.

interesting. The walk to it is good, and at the gate of the wood as we returned we had a sight of Windermere.

The next day we visited Ambleside, in order to see the Waterfall above the town, which we had heard was superior to those of Rydal.[4] We ascended the hill for some time, and at length arrived at the spot. This is far more deserving the name of a waterfall than those of Rydal, descending as we imagined about seventy feet through broken fragments of rock, and hurried from thence among loose stones, to meet the Rothay in the vale below.[5] On the 24th while two of our Companions went to the top of Helvellyn two of us went by Ambleside, across the Rothay and Brathay, along the head of Windermere to Hawkshead, nine miles from Grassmere; passing through the small village of Clappersgate in our way, where is a neat and handsome house with a fine view of the lake, the seat of Miss Pritchett or Pritchard. From this place perhaps, Windermere is seen to greater advantage than any other situation, for here it cannot be taken for a river as the observer is at the head of the lake and looks only upon its length. We passed by the little piece of water called Blellam tarn, which at first we mistook for Esthwaite water, and has nothing to recommend it.

The village of   [6] is situated nearly at the head, about a mile and an half from Hawkshead, where we soon after [7] arrived after seeing an old house, on the right of the road, called the Hall and where we conjectured was formerly the room, in which the author of the history of Furness says, the abbot of Furness received his rents from Hawkshead and kept residence by two or more of his monks.[8]

After dinner at the red Lion our Landlord directed us to the ferry at Windermere four miles from the town. Two miles of it be close to the side of Esthwaite water a lake said to be three miles in length the lower end finely border-ed with wood which, climbs almost to the tops of the hills and the upper ornamented with the town of Hawkshead, Langdale Pikes at a distance, and a beautiful swelling peninsula surrounded with trees above the tops of which we saw the green corn on its summit.

From hence we went to Sawrey a hamlet consisting of a few houses on a little hill, where on enquiring our way it was pointed out to us, by one of the most strapping women I ever beheld.

On the summit of the next hill we saw Windermere, by degrees the whole opened upon us and we saw the island

6. Gell was uncertain of the name of this village; it seems probable that it was Out Gate.

7. The time of arrival in Hawkshead has been erased.

8. Hawkshead Hall, formerly the manor house of Furness Abbey when all the land between the eastern shores of Coniston Lake and the western shores of Windermere belonged to the monastery. The gatehouse to the hall, built of local Silurian slates and New Red Sandstone brought from Low Furness, contains a room in which the manor court was held. The author of the *History of Furness* to which Gell refers was Thomas West, the writer of the first guidebook to the Lakes.

Stock Ghyll Falls by Ackermann.
'The next day we visited Ambleside,
in order to see the Waterfall above the
town, which we had heard was superior
to those of Rydal.'

The ferry across Windermere by Ackermann. 'After dinner at the red Lion our Landlord directed us to the ferry at Windermere four miles from the town.'

The west side of Windermere by Ackermann. 'On the summit of the next hill we saw Windermere, by degrees the whole opened upon us ...'

9. John Christian, of Workington Hall, an influential agriculturalist, industrialist and politician. On his marriage to Isabella Curwen he changed his name to John Christian Curwen.

10. This is a common misconception; the great east window of Bowness Church was brought from Cartmel Priory, not Furness Abbey.

11. Long Holm or Belle Isle. In 1781 the island was bought for Miss Isabella Curwen, and through her it passed to her husband, John Christian Curwen, who renamed it in honour of his wife. The strange circular house was the object of much criticism; it was originally commissioned by Mr English, the former owner of the island, but completed by the Curwens.

on which stands the house belonging to Mr. Christian,[9] in our descent to the ferry, a small house entirely overhung with trees standing on a peninsula behind which one of Mr. Christian's vessels lay at anchor. We got into a boat here in which they usually bring carts and horses across and were conveyed slowly to the other side of the lake which in this place is no more than five hundred and ten yards broad.

When we were landed we walked about half a mile to Bowness where is a window in the church taken from the abbey of Furness.[10] We hired a boat at the White Lion and were rowed by two men to Ambleside, leaving behind us the island which is entirely covered with wood forming the whole into a most delightful open grove.

This Island[11] is two miles in circumference being nearly three quarters of a mile long, and lying in a direction neither parralell to the side of the Lake nor at right angles to it. As to the house itself when the observer stands in such a position as not to percieve the portico, it wants only a little green paint and a label of Souchong or fine Hyson to make it exactly like a large shop tea canister. Sir Christopher Philipson lived in the Great island in the

beginning of the present century. How it became the property of the Curwen family I know not*.[12] It contains more than thirty acres and is in the County of Westmorland though far nearer to the Lancashire side it was anciently part of the honour of Richmond and was held by the

*I have since heard Mr. Curwen bought it of a Mr. English.

The Round House on Belle Isle, Windermere, from Plaw's Rural Architecture, 1794. *'This Island is two miles in circumference being nearly three quarters of a mile long.'*

12. Belle Isle was acquired for 1,640 guineas. (See Hughes, E., *North Country Life in the Eighteenth Century,* Volume II, Cumberland and Westmorland 1700-1830, 1965.)

*A watercolour of Rydal Water by
William Gell. 'From Ambleside we
walked to Rydal a little lake spotted
with rocky islands ...'*

Lancasters barons of Kendal. The whole lake, is ten [miles]
all but 200yds in length, the greatest breadth is not more
than 1635 yards, and the smallest not more than five hundred and ten, where the ferry is situated not far below
Bowness. The greatest depth opposite Graithwaite, is one

hundred and thirty-two feet. Opposite Rawlinsons Nab 132 feet, opposite Ecclesrig Crag 201 feet, and within one hundred yards from the conflux of the Brathay, and the Rothay, the depth is one hundred and sixty six feet.

It is remarkable that in the spawning season, Trout only

The island in Grasmere, by William Gell. 'An island rises gently about the middle of the water, except that on the south west side the shore is rocky and one or two rows of firs contribute to the abruptness of the appearance.'

13. This is incorrect: trout ascend both the Rothay and the Brathay, and, although char are more common in the Brathay, they are also found in the Rothay. Similarly, Gell's story of the underwater current in Windermere is fictitious. I am indebted to Dr H C Gilson of the Freshwater Biological Laboratory, Ferry House, Far Sawrey, for this information.

14. Richard Watson, bishop of Llandaff, was a Cumbrian by birth. He was appointed to the Chair of Chemistry in the university of Cambridge in 1764, though he knew virtually nothing of the subject. In 1771, after shameless political manoeuvring, he was appointed to the Regius Chair of Divinity, and in 1782 was consecrated Bishop of Llandaff. Shortly after his appointment to the see, he built Calgarth and spent most of his remaining years there living the life of a country squire. He died in 1816.

15. The macabre legend of the Calgarth skulls is associated with Calgarth Hall, the Elizabethan mansion of the Philipson family.

ascend the Rothay and Char the Brathay.[13] The fishermen affirm that before any great storm there is a current under water exactly opposite to the direction in which the storm will appear; this we had not an opportunity of observing though the water was ruffled so violently that we apprehended an approaching storm. Calgarth the seat of the Bishop of Llandaff [14] is situated on a gently rising ground on the right, an handsome stone mansion, at a small distance from the old hall, where are preserved the famous skulls, of which it is reported, that they have been burnt, ground, powdered and cast into the lake, but nevertheless have constantly returned to the window in which they first lay as a perpetual testimony, of the innocence of their original owners, who were executed on suspicion of a murder, which they never committed.[15]

After passing Low wood Inn, we arrived at Ambleside and borded not far from the Camp which the Romans formed at the head of Windermere and which commanded a view as far down the lake as the holme. The dimensions were 396 feet by 240, no Military road has yet been discovered leading to it, though many of the learned in Antiquities, have taken much trouble, and some have written dissertations on the subject.[16] The fall at the lower end of this lake, from Newby bridge where it terminates, to Low wood bridge is one hundred and five feet, at Low wood bridge the tide rises some inches or feet.

Mr. Curwen the present proprietor of the Holme, was formerly a Christian, but having married the heiress of the Curwen family and bringing by her between fifteen and twenty thousand pounds annually into his own changed his name for that of his lady. (I believe this partly untrue.) The Curwens themselves were originally descended from Gospatric from whom also the Nevils' Earls of Westmorland were derived, but on marrying the heiress of the Curwens of Galloway in Scotland they took the name which they have ever since retained. They had anciently a seat at Workington near Cockermouth and the present Mr. Curwen has made considerable improvements there*.

From Ambleside we walked to Rydal a little lake spotted with rocky islands, two or three of which are cloathed with wood but not of sufficient extent to become an object of attention in a countrey abounding with so many superior:

16. The Roman fort of Galava, on the delta of the rivers Rothay and Brathay, seems to have been originally built about AD 79 or 80. The ramparts were of earth and clay, and the buildings were wooden. The fort was surrounded by a double ditch. It appears that this camp was voluntarily evacuated, possibly because its low-lying position made it particularly liable to flooding. However, sometime between AD 100 and AD 120 the site was re-occupied and the fort rebuilt in stone on an artificially-created platform. It survived for approximately 250 years, though not without incident, for it was attacked and damaged by fire on several occasions. Gell's remarks about the Roman road are interesting, for they show that even as early as 1797 the route of this road was being sought; in spite of fieldwork and such sophisticated techniques as aerial photography, the exact course of the road between the Roman fort at Watercrook, south of Kendal, and Galava remains uncertain. (See Rollinson, William, *A History of Man in the Lake District*, 1967; and Hindle, Paul, *Roads and Tracks of the Lake District*, 1998.)

---

*Curwens arms Ar frettè Gu a chief az.

Wyburn Water (Thirlmere)
by Ackermann.

Grassmere is but little more than a mile from Rydal and from the hill between the two lakes, is one of the best views of the whole valley Lake and Island that I have seen.

The lake itself is small, the village is a little way from the head consisting a of few houses, and a white church situate close to the bridge over the Rothay which is the principal feeder of the lake. We lodged at Robert Newton's[17] at the Red Lion where there is a comfortable house, and we experienced very civil treatment. We had a boat on the meer at our pleasure. An island rises gently about the middle of the water, except that on the south west side the shore is rocky and one or two rows of firs contribute to the abruptness of the appearance. A small barn or perhaps a shelter for cattle is on the extremity, the whole measures about four acres and an half. There are a few Rabbits among the rocks.

Towards Keswick, the piramidal hill called helm Crag, Steel fell and Seat Sandal, are the boundaries of this peaceful valley and shut out all beyond. The church within is miserable, one or two hatchments as I suppose of the Knott's of Rydal hang on the damp green walls.[18] In the second window from the altar is an oval of stained glass

17. Robert Newton's inn, the Red Lion, was famed for its hospitality. In 1792, Joseph Budworth enjoyed a gargantuan meal there which included:
  'Roast pike, stuffed
  A boiled fowl
  Veal-cutlets and ham Beans and bacon
  Cabbage
  Pease and potatoes Anchovy sauce
  Parsley and butter Plain butter
  Butter and cheese
  Wheat bread and oat cake
  Three cups of preserved gooseberries, with a bowl of rich cream in the centre; For two people, at ten-pence per head'
(see *A Fortnight's Ramble to the Lakes,* by 'A Rambler' (Joseph Budworth), 1792.)

18 St Oswald's Grasmere, like most of the dales churches, was an unpretentious building:
  'Not raised in nice proportion was the pile
  But large and messy, for duration built'
    Wordsworth, *The Prelude,* Book 5.
Until 1840 the floor remained unpaved, and rushes were collected from the lakeside to strew on the earth floor. This, of course, is the origin of the Grasmere Rush Bearing ceremony.

19. Duvenald or Dunmail, the last British king of Cumbria, was defeated in AD 945 by King Edmund of Northumbria. There are several legends associated with the battle and the pile of stones on the summit of the pass, but it is believed that Dunmail died in Rome several years after the battle.

20. Leathes Water, an alternative name for Thirlmere. The Leathes family built Dale Head Hall in 1623.

with the same.* On the 27th of June we all four set out from Grassmere for Keswick passing the heap of stones in the way called Dunmail raise which were piled together by one of the Saxon Edmunds in order to commemorate his victory over Dunmail the last king of Cumberland.[19] The heap is not large perhaps 15 yards across over the top is built the wall which divides the Counties of Cumberland and Westmorland. From dunmail raise we saw the lake of Leatheswater[20] and as we descended the hill the base of Helvellyn stretched along the right of the road. Leathes water is about two miles and ½ in length; in breadth no where much more than a quarter as it appeared to me. After crossing the Greeta the little romantic vale of St. John is just caught to the right, but from the village of Legberthwaite till within one or two miles of Keswick nothing is worthy attention or in the smallest degree interesting except Skiddow and Saddleback at a distance.

From Grassmere to Keswick is twelve miles. About half a mile above the latter we had a most delightful view of the vale, the town, the lake of Bassenthwaite and part of

*Gu a fren Ar crest on a wreath or [indistinct] knot Az.

Derwent. We lodged at the Queens head, Mr. Woods and were received with every attention we could wish. We went that evening to Crosthwaites museum.

Looking north on the road from Ambleside to Keswick, engraved by Farington.

His collection chiefly consists of mineral productions and those indian bows, caps, and ornaments which are to be found in every museum. He had a collection of coins,

21. Peter Crosthwaite, like Joseph Pocklington, was one of the most colourful characters in eighteenth-century Cumbria. After a period in the service of the East India Company, he became a customs officer at Blyth in Northumberland, but returned to his native Cumberland in 1779 and in 1780 opened his famous museum *(pictured above)* in the Square at Keswick. But this was not his sole interest, for in 1783 he began to produce the first of a series of maps of the major lakes, the waterfalls and cascades, and the houses of the 'Gentry' — in short, all that was likely to interest the tourist. His methods of attracting visitors to his museum can hardly have found favour with his neighbours, but they nevertheless mark the beginnings of an important new industry in the Lake District — commercial tourism. (See Crosthwaite, P, *A Series of Accurate Maps of the Principal Lakes of Cumberland, Westmorland and Lancashire,* facsimile edition 1968, with an introduction and notes by William Rollinson.)

which I did not examine, the chair of Ld Derwentwater, a chinese Gong which produced a most thundering sound, and an instrument of the staccato kind, made of stone of which he pretends to have found six notes in the proper musical succession. He[21] also sells his own maps of the lakes which have the character of the nicest accuracy in every respect. His daughter seems an elegant woman, and more worth seeing than any thing else in his house, as to himself he is seated in a gouty chair and drums in one corner of the room, like a fool, to the noise of a barrel organ. While he has mirrors in every direction at the windows, by which he instantly sees every carriage that comes from any of the neighbouring towns, though he sits not near to any of the windows himself. The organ strikes up if any one passes, and his horrible drum is thumped, at the same time that the old woman runs upstairs and rattles away at the Gong, in a manner that cannot fail to attract the notice of the unfortunate strangers in the street. He has even attempted to make a larger Gong than that he has already, with which he might astonish strangers but this has not succeeded, probably owing to the too great thickness of the brass of which it is formed.

On the 28th I rambled by the side of the lake; and fortunately hit on a most advantageous spot for seeing at one view the whole of the lake, its islands and the

'A View of Derwentwater towards Borrodale' by William Bellers. One 'of the earliest picturesque views of the Lake District' (Bicknell).

22. Gell was clearly much impressed by the view of Derwentwater and Borrowdale from Friars Crag, a view which John Ruskin was later to describe as being among the three or four most beautiful scenes in Europe.

surrounding mountains. It is called Friar's Crag[22] where you may place yourself in such a manner as to see most of the beauties of the lake, yet not be disgusted with the folly and childishness of what is now called Pocklingtons island, where is an house that appears to have dropped from the clouds, one or two batteries with pasteboard battlements and a spruceness in the whole, which cannot accord in any degree with the surrounding scenery.

Exactly opposite the Crag is an island called Lord island from having been formerly the occasional residence of the Radcliff's Earls of Derwentwater, who took their title from this lake. The first of this family who appears to have been mentioned in history, was Sir Nicholas Radcliffe of Dilston in the County of Northumberland Knight, in the time of Edward the first, whose descendant married the heiress of the Derwentwaters in the time of Henry the Sixth, and through her obtained this princely estate. Francis first Earl of Derwentwater his lineal descendant, became Baron Dilston Viscount Langley and Radcliff and Earl of Derwentwater in the time of King James the second, but his son adhering to the unfortunate family of Stewart, on their attempt to recover the throne in the year 1716,[23] lost at

23. Although the Jacobite Rebellion lasted until 1716, it is more usual to ascribe it to 1715.

once his titles estate and life. It is I believe certain that his brother left issue abroad, as to himself, coming over in the late unfortunate and unsuccessful struggle of Prince Charles in the year forty five, he was seized and convicted upon his former attainder, without any enquiry as to his conduct on the latter occasion, but merely as to the assistance he gave to his Brother in 1716. It is the belief of the vulgar that some years ago a young man of genteel appearance came to see this Lake, with a friend who acted as interpreter, as he himself could not speak English. They enquired for an old man in Keswick, who served them as a guide, and desired to see all that ever belonged to the Derwentwater family, he took them upon one of the neighbouring hills and pointed out to them as accurately as he was able every part of the Estate which lay before them, the young man burst into tears. Afterwards having handsomely rewarded his conductor he turned away from the scene and quitted the kingdom immediately. He is supposed to have been of the Radcliff family, and probably from the younger brother of the attainted Earl before mentioned. Camden says this family had anciently a castle at Castle Rigg and adds that the fine old oaks which surrounded

24. The Greenwich Hospital acquired the forfeited Derwentwater estate in 1735, and the trustees felled and sold the oaks to James Spedding for £5,300. Gell had probably consulted the 1772 or 1789 edition of Camden's *Britannia*.

25. Here the words 'rather a lie' are added as an afterthought.

26. Pocklington's eccentricities took various forms. As well as organising regattas and arranging mock 'sea-battles' on Derwentwater, he busied himself in other ways. He diverted the flow of water over Barrow Cascade, while at the Bowder Stone in Borrowdale, he built a small cottage and installed an old woman who acted as guide to visitors. He even had a hole cut in the base of the great boulder so that, in the words of Southey, 'the curious may gratify themselves by shaking hands with the old woman.'

the mansion were cut down by the trustees of the Grenwich hospital to the maintenance of which the forfeited estate was applied.[24] The present representative in England receives at present no more than two thousand five hundred pounds annually, although the estate amounts to more than 20,000, and it is remarkable that of the Fraser's and others who were concerned at the same time with Ld Derwentwater every one has had their property restored except this family. Pocklingtons Island is like all which formerly belonged to the Radcliff's let upon long leases to the different[25] tennants. The taste of Mr. Pocklington in buildings and decorations, is so remarkable that I cannot omit to mention a few of his singularities.[26] On making the foundation for his cellars and house at the island, was found a great stone, this, though the Architect wished it to remain, as an excellent foundation, he resolved to fix upright before his house and at a great expence had it placed there. A druid temple was the next thing to employ his genius and accordingly he collected a number of large stones, placed them in a circle, and had them fixed upright on the southern shore. Unfortunately for all the lovers of British antiquity a storm arose in the lake, and the waves

*Pocklington's Island on Derwentwater.
'… the folly and childishness of what is
now called Pocklingtons island, where
is an house that appears to have
dropped from the clouds …'*

Facing page: Peter Crosthwaite's map of Pocklington's Island, 1783.
'The taste of Mr. Pocklington in buildings and decorations, is so remarkable that I cannot omit to mention a few of his singularities ...'

27. Peter Crosthwaite's map of the island, 1809 edition, records that it passed to Peachy in 1796. Later, it reverted to its former name, Vicars Island.

washed down in one night the labours of some days. On the other side a venerable whitewashed gothic building rears its august head, in all the pride of pasteboard antiquity. A church, Faro batteries and four or five cannon painted white make up the whole of this miraculous assemblage of beauties, and surround the enchanted island, I say enchanted for tis plain nature never formed in her most sportive moments, such an awkward jumble of fantastic gew gaws.

He has just sold this spot to Mr. Peachy[27] and means to retire to Barrow cascade hall, where if possible he has outdone himself in ridiculous fancies. The house is not very particular but a white embattled hermitage is situated on an eminence near it, where he has offered half a crown a day to anyone who will live in it, provided the wretch will submit to his conditions, which are these. The hermit is never to leave the place, or hold conversation with anyone for 7 years during which time he is neither to wash himself or cleanse himself in any way whatever, but is to let his hair and nails both on hands and feet, grow as long as nature will permit them. Though the reward is certainly great, yet the happiness of the situation is such that he has never yet been able to persuade any one to accept his

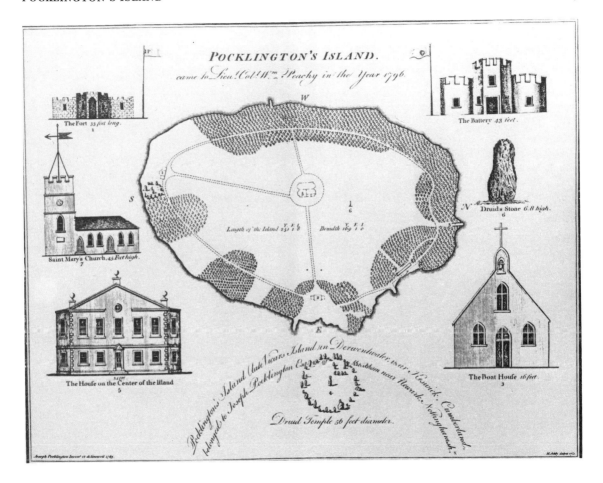

POCKLINGTON'S ISLAND.

came to Lieut. Colt. Wm. Peachy in the Year 1796.

The Fort 33 feet long.
1

The Battery 43 feet.

Saint Mary's Church. 45 Feet high.
7

Druids Stone 6.8 high.
6

The House on the Center of the Island
5

The Boat House 16 feet.
3

Length of the Island 251 ⅓
Breadth 169 ⅓

Pocklington's Island (late Vicars Island) in Derwentwater, near Keswick, Cumberland, belonged to Joseph Pocklington Esqr. Grasham near Keswick, Nottinghamds.

Druid Temple 56 feet diameter.

Joseph Pocklington Inven. et delineavit 1783.

28. Hermits became fashionable in the eighteenth century; they were part of the Romantic movement and an important component of the Picturesque scene. At Conishead, an early nineteenth-century mansion on the site of a medieval priory overlooking Morecambe Bay, Colonel T R G Braddyll employed a hermit for the amusement of his guests. The man is said to have held the post for twenty years, during which time his nails and hair remained uncut.

29. It is assumed that the author was here referring to Lord's Island, once the home of the Radcliffe family.

30. Unfortunately a page has been removed from the manuscript at this point. Previously Gell had questioned the retention of the Derwentwater Estate when other forfeited lands had been restored to the owners, and it might be supposed that he recorded a protest in his manuscript but later thought better of it and removed the page.

31. William Gell was a member of a famous Derbyshire family.

proposals.[28] In short all his white buildings and ornaments contribute to diminish the simple beauty of the lake, which is without exception otherwise the finest piece of water I have yet seen in these parts.

While I sat under the rocks of friar crag, and looked at the island,[29] once the seat of hospitality but now deserted and long since covered with wood, the following thoughts came into my head and had I not been interrupted, they would have been written on the rocks which are just opposite to Lowdore, at that time destitute of water, and remarkable from that distance only ...[30] I was suddenly surprized by the sound of a female voice on the crag above me, looking up I saw a gentleman and a lady with whom I soon became acquainted and found that they were Mr. Aufrere and his lady who had known my relations in Derbyshire.[31] I found him a very agreeable and entertaining man, and Mrs. Aufrere an elegant woman. They gave me much information on the subject of Keswick, and its environs.

After dinner we took a boat and landed on Pocklingtons Island, where having laughed sufficiently, we rowed between Lords Island and the shore where our rowers informed us though I know not on what grounds there had been a draw bridge to connect it with the mainland.[32] Not a vestige of the house remains except perhaps a small part of the foundation scarcely visible it was destroyed by the Duke of Cumberland's forces in 1716.[33]

There is a tradition among the vulgar, that a chest of gold of great value was thrown into the lake by Ld Derwentwater's order before he went to the assistance of the Stewarts, this is probably merely one of the romances which usually attend everything of this kind. From thence we landed at St. Herberts island where that saint is reputed to have prayed and obtained his desire to die the same day hour and minute with his former friend and preceptor St. Cuthbert, who if I mistake not died at the abbey of Lindisfarne in holy island opposite the mouth of the tyne. I like it far better than the others; both Pocklingtons and Lords islands are much too near the shore, while this is but little less than half a mile from the very nearest point of the mainland. They showed us what they thought or pretended to believe, the remains of St. Herbert's cell, but he had a good notion of building without mortar, if he could make it last from his own time to this, and indeed did not spare

32. There is no evidence to support such a theory.

33. Here Gell is factually incorrect. It is most likely that the house was dismantled during the Civil War, and certainly by 1709 it was in ruins. (See Robinson, T, *Natural History of Cumberland and Westmorland,* 1709; also Collingwood, W G, 'The Home of the Derwentwaters', *Trans Cumberland and Westmorland Antiquarian and Archaeological Society,* new series, volume 4, 1904.)

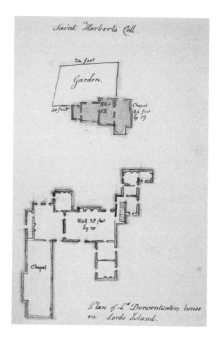

William Gell's plans of St Herbert's Cell (top) and Lord Derwentwater's house on Lord's Island. 'They showed us what they thought or pretended to believe, the remains of St. Herbert's cell, but he had a good notion of building without mortar, if he could make it last from his own time to this …'

either time, or labour, in erecting a building of such an extent, if it were possible the present building could be really his.[34] The whole is most beautifully covered with trees and a walk to the southern extremity is overhung with lofty pines. Its only inhabitant is a poor jack ass, who if he has the spirit of contemplation within him may here turn anchorite and enjoy himself in his unenvied solitude. We next landed at Lowdore where we had a nearer view of what may sometimes be a most roaring cataract, but when we saw it had not so much water as the little falls of Rydal. From Lowdore to Grange is a pleasant walk of two miles, where we endeavoured to procure a lodging at the village, just at the entrance of Borrowdale, but did not succeed. We saw the famous Bowdar Stone a little farther about 21 yards in length and eleven high a most enormous mass weighing upwards of 1771 tons.[35]

Castle Crag, rises in a piramidal form, on its summit once was a castle, few however if any traces of it now remain.[36] We determined to proceed along the vale to Buttermere, although we had nine or ten miles to go, and to use the expression of the countrymen one of the blindest roads we could have chosen.

A little after we passed the village of Rosthwaite, we began to ascend a steep hill which with much time and labour we at last overcame.[37] Hitherto I had seen nothing equal to Dovedale,[38] and here though by far the most romantic part of the country, the hills wanted the spiry rocks and the valley the transparent steam, to render it worthy of comparison. The account of it in West's guide, though not written by himself is as much overcharged in this subject as it is generally on every other. From the last ascent, we found a most surprising view down a deep valley, enclosed on either side by lofty crags, and almost covered below with huge fragments of rock that seemed to have been rent from the surrounding heights. We saw one which we judged might even be one quarter the size of the great Bowdar but in this we might probably be deceived[39] as darkness began to overtake us, and the road became so rugged that any attention to the scenery of the country, must have been attended by a stumble over some of the pointed slate of which the way is composed. A few trifling slips gave us warning of what we had to expect without care, and we afterwards heard that a guide from Keswick had broken his leg there, about a year before we visited the spot.

34. In the fourteenth century the cult of St. Herbert, a seventh-century hermit, was revived, and for a time the island in Derwentwater became a centre for pilgrimages. A small chapel was built there, possibly on the site of the saint's original cell, and it seems likely that Gell saw the remains of this building.

35. This is the figure which West gives in his *Guide to the Lakes*.

36. West mentions a fort on the summit and suggests that it 'has most likely been of Roman origin, to guard the pass and secure the treasure contained in the bosom of the mountains', but from its form it appears to have been some kind of Dark Age refuge.

37. Honister Pass.

38. Dovedale in Derbyshire.

39. A pencilled note in a different hand, perhaps Buswick Harwood's, declares: 'Gell, thou wert deceiv'd by the Darkness of Night'

*The Bowder Stone and Castle Crag,
Borrowdale, by William Gell. 'We saw
the famous Bowdar Stone a little
farther about 21 yards in length and
eleven high a most enormous mass
weighing upwards of 1771 tons.'*

Buttermere Lake *(1798) by J M W Turner. 'At length we saw buttermere; at the head of the lake stand two or three houses ...' (© Tate, London 2000.)*

Buttermere Hawse. '… the road became nothing more than a morass …'

A short time before we arrived at the top of the fell the road became nothing more than a morass, and it is curious to relate that a dispute ensued, whether a loose line of stones on which we stood was intended for a road or the

bed of a torrent at the time when a considerable fall of ruin, or the dissolution of winter snows, produces frequent floods in this mountainous region. At length we saw buttermere; at the head of the lake stand two or three houses, called Gatesgarth, where we learnt from a man who answered our question from his bed, that we only wanted two miles of the village. We entered the village at eleven, and at the door of the inn, known only by the name of Joseph Robinsons,[40] for there is no sign, we were received by the

The Fish Inn, Buttermere.
'We entered the village at eleven,
and at the door of the inn, known
only by the name of Joseph
Robinson, for there is no sign,
we were received by the landlords
daughter, the celebrated beauty
of those parts.'

40. The inn was the Fish.

41. Mary Robinson, 'the Beauty of Buttermere' *(pictured above)*. After Joseph Budworth first drew attention to Mary's charm and good looks in his book *A Fortnight's Tour to the Lakes* of 1792, the tourists began to arrive from Keswick to see this famed beauty for themselves — Gell and his party included. In 1802, Mary married the 'Hon Colonel Hope', but alas he was neither honourable nor a colonel, for he was John Hatfield, a notorious forger and bigamist. He was hanged in Carlisle the following year and Mary became a *cause célèbre*. Fortunately the story had a happy ending, for Mary Robinson married again and went with her husband to live at Caldbeck. See Melvyn Bragg's novel *The Maid of Buttermere*, 1987.

landlords daughter, the celebrated beauty of those parts.[41] While our good old hostess, prepared our beds the lovely daughter waited on us at supper, with that good nature and attention which soon determined us as much in favour of her disposition, as we were before captivated by the charms of her person. Indeed so much attention was paid us, that we all agreed to remain at Buttermere some days, though our original intention was to have left it the day after our arrival. We saw the amazing fall of Scale force in the course of the next day, and it is indeed worthy of notice, falling precipitately from the summit of the hill into a chasm scarce six yards wide enclosed on every side but the outlet, by rocks which in some places start up in perpendicular masses and in others hang over in a manner that joined to the height of one hundred and fifty feet perpendicular render the whole tremendous and unrivalled. It is indeed worthy the pencil of a Rosa, the trees covered with moss, the fern starting up in the angles of the rock, and the dashing of the water are highly finished much in his stile. There are two falls, the lower not more than twelve feet in height, nature has left a kind of staircase by the side of it which seems to have been improved by art

*A sketch of Scale Force by William Gell.
'Scale force ... is indeed worthy of
notice, falling precipitately from the
summit of the hill into a chasm scarce
six yards wide enclosed on every side
but the outlet, by rocks ...'*

in order to give a full view of the higher fall, which otherwise could not have been obtained.

Some days after we climbed the steep hill above the village of Buttermere and saw the lakes of Loweswater Crommock and Buttermere on one side with Pocklingtons island and Derwentwater, Newlands vale, and the rudest assemblage of hills, and rocks, I ever beheld on the other.

We even imagined we saw the sea over Mell break, an hill on the side of Crummock. Buttermere is two miles, Crummock about three, and Loweswater just one mile in length, where the hills are softened to rising grounds and the tameness of the scene cannot please, when the eye has been accustomed to the wildness of Buttermere.

On Sunday the second of July we went to church and were reconciled to our miserable situation with damp walls and wet soil, for there is no floor,[42] by the sight of a large number of attendants for the size of the place, and the appearance of a respectable preacher. The daughter of our host was our conductress. In the night it rained so hard that every little rill became a torrent or waterfall, we wished to re-visit scale force but fishing or other amusements prevented us for sometime.

42. The poverty of the dale churches is not really surprising. As late as 1845, the floor of Wasdale Head chapel was covered with bracken, and there were only two pews, the rest of the seats being sheep forms on trestles.

On Tuesday the fourth of July we gave a dance to the villagers of Buttermere, our company consisted of five and thirty persons and if it be a pleasure to see merry faces and good humour we had them here in perfection. We regaled the ladies with queen cakes and punch the rest with ale and porter and for the little expence of perhaps half a guinea on each of us we gave an entertainment unequalled in the annals of Buttermere. We danced from eight in the evening till two the next morning between each country dance, the customary gigs of the country took place for it is usual for every one to ask each of the females to dance a gig though there be thirty in company. We saw scale force again some days after, my companions thought it improved, by the addition of a considerable flood, for my own part I thought the height appeared so much diminished, as to take away greatly from the effect.

We went to Cockermouth on the seventh, saw the castle a small and never apparently a strong building, founded by Waltheof son to Gospatric, lord of Allerdale. Over the gate are the arms of Molton, Humfranville Lucy and Percy as Camden says but he forgets to mention the fifth shield, the coat of the Nevill's who married the heiress of Gospatric

Cockermouth Castle, from William Gell's journal. '… a small and never apparently a strong building …'

43. A Roman altar is built into the north side of the gatehouse. (See Collingwood, W G, *The Lake Counties*, 1932.)

Earl of Northumberland during the reign of the Conqueror, or soon after. This Castle is reported to have been built from the ruins of the Roman Papcastle, by the Britons called Palmcastle, a short distance from Cockermouth.[43]

The town itself is not large, and has little to recommend

it. The name is taken from the situation, standing on the conflux of the Rivers Cocker, and Derwent. The site of this castle, is now the property of the Earl of Egremont who derives his title, from another castle in this county, founded by William de Meschines Earl of Chester, whose daughter married William fitz Duncan, of the blood Royal of Scotland, from whom the title passed through the families of Lucy, Molton, and Fitzwalter, till it came to the Radcliff's Earls of Sussex. Thos. Percy in the reign of Henry the sixth, was first Lord of Egremont, of that family, and I believe the present posessor of Cockermouth is his descendant.

We returned to Buttermere the next day, passing through Lorton, where is perhaps the largest school in the county, if that of St. Bees be excepted, which is situated on the coast, and so called from St. Bega one of those ladies who came to seek their fortunes here from Ireland, which indeed was much the fashion of those days, for we read of St. Winifred and at least a dozen others from that country, doing the same. This virgin is said to have tamed a wild bull, by her piety, and to have covered the hills and vallies of Cumberland with snow, in the midst of summer[44] but

44. The medieval legend of St Bees concerns a certain Celtic saint, Bega and her nuns, who landed on the shores of West Cumberland and begged the lord of the manor for land on which to found a church. He granted to them as much land as the snow covered at midsummer, and of course snow fell on midsummer's day. There can be no doubt that there existed at this spot a pre-Norman church with an Irish name, Kirkby Begog, a name probably introduced by Christianised Norse-Irish settlers. See Melvyn Bragg's novel *Credo*, 1996.

Gell's depiction of Crummock Water. 'We rowed that evening on the lake of Crummock, a most delightfully glowing sunset, tinged the water, and the surrounding mountains, with the finest purple we had ever seen.'

the question whether she deserved to be canonized for the latter piece of mischief, if left to the good people whose land she injured, would more probably have been determined, in favour of burning her for a witch, than raising her to the skies. From Lorton to Buttermere is about seven miles, the road tolerable to Buttermere hawse,

a rock jutting out a little way into Crommock, and we were happy to find that our arrival at Buttermere was as pleasing as it was unexpected to the inhabitants of the village. We rowed that evening on the lake of Crummock, a most delightfully glowing sunset, tinged the water, and the surrounding mountains, with the finest purple we had ever seen. We landed at Holme island, and afterwards at Bowmans island where we sat some time building aerial castles on the rock, while we enjoyed the scene. It was one of the finest evenings we had seen since the commencement of our tour. The island we found to be about forty four yards

Bowmans Island on Crummock Water, and its imaginary castle, as pictured by William Gell. '… at Bowmans island … we sat some time building aerial castles on the rock, while we enjoyed the scene. It was one of the finest evenings we had seen since the commencement of our tour.'

45. Here, several sentences have been obliterated by black ink or paint *(see above)*. Although in some places the surface of the paper has been removed, it is possible to decipher the following using ultra-violet light: '… little were they acquainted with the name of vice that the very circumstances of staying behind in the other served to show off in greater lustre the purity of the daughter of our land lord and her companion'. Following these words is the pencilled comment 'ha ha ha, W.G.'

long, perhaps twenty in breadth. The whole is covered with wood like the Holme and bilberries grow plentifully on each. Some evenings after we rowed two of the village maidens and a friend of theirs whose nicer feelings, for she had been educated at Cockermouth, could neither bear the motion of the boat, or the landing on the New island where the grass was not perfectly free from dew. New island is hardly fifty yards from the shore and somewhat larger than either of the others. Wood house island is a fourth where we landed, and finding great quantities of bilberries we sat down on the grass and regaled ourselves while the lady in the boat amused herself by her own thoughts on the occasion …[45]

The day after we visited Ennerdale water over five miles of fells and bogs. A mist prevented us from seeing the lake for some time but on clearing up a fine piece of water and a rude fell on the opposite shore rewarded us for our trouble. There is one small island situated about the middle of the lake. We left this retired spot on the …… of July, I believe we may without vanity assert that all to whom we were known were not a little sorry at our departure, nor were we on our part insensible to the kindness

Ennerdale Water by William Gell.
'A mist prevented us from seeing the
lake for some time but on clearing up
a fine piece of water and a rude fell on
the opposite shore rewarded us for our
trouble.'

and hospitality of these our rustic friends. We passed the lofty Grassmire on the left, scarce ten yards are wanting to make this mountain, equal to Skiddaw in height,[46] its colour is remarkable being of a tawny hue, without any covering except here and there a speck of heath to diversify its appearance. On the right just below Robinsons Crag and exactly at the head of Newlands vale is a waterfall, the height of the rock we did not recollect to observe.

The author of the guide to the lakes found a beauty and wildness in the valley of Newlands which I believe others will scarce imagine with the assistance of the most romantic

46. Grasmoor is 2,791 feet high, Skiddaw 3,053 feet.

47. Portinscale House in Finckle Street, later passed to Lord William Gordon who re-named it Derwent Bank.

genius they can summon for the occasion. The upper end of the valley is poor and if the lower part has any thing particular to attract the attention ours certainly must have been employed another way during our walk. It was with some difficulty we passed a rapid stream at Braithwaite where we left the road and crossed a few fields towards Portinscale a village not far from Keswick. We endeavoured in our way, to catch the sound of Lowdore from the opposite side of Derwentwater but a neighbouring river rolling among loose stones prevented us. At a place called Fincle street in Portinscale Mr. Pocklington has built another of his elegant villas,[47] the situation is good, commanding a view of both Bassenthwaite and Derwentwaters, but all situations may lose much of their effect, by the erection of a tall thin white house, round the angles and windows, of which, runs an elegant border of dirty red, which renders it infinitely more rual and agrees charmingly with the truely romantic, and engaging scenery of Derwent. There is however this comfort that his houses are so slightly built that the people think they cannot stand long to be the eye sores of the lake.

We had the good fortune to see the effect of what is

called in this country a bottom wind proceeding from some hitherto unknown cause or at least so far uncertain that there are many different opinions on the subject. The appearance is nearly as I can describe it was this. One part was agitated violently without the least apparent cause, while another was so smooth as to have scarcely move than a ripple upon its surface, a boat with two men was tossed up and down in a storm in one part while a man at no great distance was fishing quietly with a rod and line from another. There was little if any wind stirring at the time, and the waves seemed to make more noise than they would if equally agitated in the usual way. I am not certain whether this phenominon is peculiar to this lake, at present I have heard of it in no other. We lodged at our former inn the Queens head, and found every convenience and attention we required.

In the morning we set out for Ullswater intending to take Graystoke and Dacre Castles in our way. Soon after we had passed the first mile stone we got over an hedge to the right and saw the Druids temple,[48] a circle of stones none of which are more than eight feet in height, the diameter of the whole I have forgotten. We were now on

48. The Castlerigg Circle, near Keswick, an early Bronze Age megalithic monument. The misconception that these circles were 'Druids' Temples' has remained until the present, and although the exact purpose of these monuments remains shrouded in mystery, we can be sure that they were built long before the Druids. However, the Druids fitted well enough into the Picturesque and the Romantic, and consequently the circle was visited by many of the early tourists. It is known that John Keats visited the site, and perhaps this prompted him to write in *Hyperion* of gods:

' … like a dismal cirque
Of Druid stones, upon a forlorn moor
When the chill rain begins at shut of eve,
In dull November, and their chancel vault,
The heaven itself, is blinded throughout night.'

Castlerigg Stone Circle. '...saw the Druids temple, a circle of stones none of which are more than eight feet in height ...'

the Penrith road and in passing through the vale of St. John which in that part has nothing worthy attention, the sun shone with such heat as obliged us to walk but slowly, till we had travelled eight miles of our way. Not far from the tenth mile stone we turned to the left through the small village of Penruddock to Graystock castle which we judged to be about four miles from the turnpike road. While our eggs and bacon were preparing at a small house in Graystoke we walked to the castle situated in a park well stocked with deer and the property of the Duke of Norfolk, it is perhaps one of the most retired situations in the kingdom.

The dutchess has resided here for more than three years and seldom stirs from the walls of the castle. The present building is neither new nor is it the ancient castle but was by the appearance probably erected about the begginning of the present century. The rooms are not large and seem but half furnished an handsome oak stair-case conducts you to the upper story where on seeing dust curtains hanging from the top of the room, we expected to have found some of the richly worked hangings usually concealed behind them, but I believe our surprize was very visible to the housekeeper who pulling the cover aside discovered nothing but a common cotton bed in the new style from which we immediately turned. There is one of blue velvet stiffened with silver in an adjoining room, the embroidery no doubt executed by some of the noble ladies of the Howard family, this has no cover, though for richness it far surpasses the others and must have cost ten times the sum, at the time it was made. The front of this building represented in Grose, and in a set of engravings by Byrne has been taken down by the present duke. Leaving Graystock we proceeded to Dacre Castle once the seat of the Dacre family who had great possessions in the north. Dumbrough Castle and Burgh belonged to them. The last given by one of the earls of Chester to Robt. de Trivers from whom it came to the Morvilles one of whom forfeited it by the murder of Thos a Becket in 1170 as well as his castle of Brougham. Brougham is about three miles from Penrith and I sincerely regret that our time did not permit us to see the notable ruins. In the time of the conqueror it belonged to Hugo de Albinois from the Morvilles the Viponts succeeded to it in whose time part was demolished. The famous Countess of Pembroke[49] once possessed it and during a visit here a great part of the Arcadia of Sir Philip Sidney was written. With respect to the Dacre family all that I can at present recollect is that by the marriage of Ranulph Lord Dacre with Maud, daughter and heir of one of the Multons which family had the

49. Lady Anne Clifford, sole heiress of George Clifford, third earl of Cumberland. Lady Anne married Richard Sackville, earl of Dorset, and after his death the earl of Pembroke, a nephew of Sir Philip Sidney. She did much to repair the damage of the Civil War, restoring the castles at Skipton, Pendragon, Brougham, Appleby, Brough and Barden Tower, as well as several churches.

representatives of the Morvilles and Vaulx's of Gillesland the title of Gillesland and the great possessions of the three families came to the Dacres. There were two families one called Dacre of the north and the other of Gillesland.

Dacre Castle by William Gell. 'Leaving Graystock we proceeded to Dacre Castle once the seat of the Dacre family who had great possessions in the north.'

The part which now remains, I conjecture to have been no more than the keep of the ancient castle. It is at present the property of the Hassels of Dalemain about two miles distant. We had a view of it from the towers of Dacre. Dalemain was anciently part of the barony of Graystock and held as Camden says of that lordship in cornage. We found the people at the castle civil and obliging and they gave us milk, and one of the fairest married women in the kingdom, conducted us to the top of the building through a narrow stone staircase. From hence we walked perhaps two miles, to Pooley bridge in our way passing by one side of the hill Dunmallet, till we arrived at the side of Ulleswater where some fishermen who said they belonged to the duke of Norfolk sold us three pounds of their trout and Grayling which we carried to the inn and dressed for supper. There are two public houses in the village, we found at Prichardsons a very decent lodging. We were now on the ...[50] side of Dunmallet and with some difficulty ascended to its summit, not on account of its height but the steepness of the path. This hill is situated exactly at the lower end of Ulleswater and on one side the ...[51] takes its course from the lake on the other the ...[52] The view

50, 51, 52. Here the author leaves gaps in the manuscript.

Ullswater by Ackermann. '... the scenery round the lake was as rich as a fine sheet of water and woods and fruitful enclosures down to the waters edge could make it ...'

53. The so-called Roman station was probably a hill fort, perhaps built by the Celtic peoples during the fourth century, when the power of Rome was declining and attacks by sea raiders from Ireland became more frequent. The ramparts on the summit of Dunmallet, like those at Castlehow on the shores of Bassenthwaite Lake, have a closer affinity with Dark Age fortification than with the regular and symmetrical camps of the Romans.

54. The nunnery is a figment of a fine Gothic imagination, for there is no evidence of such a building on the summit of Dunmallet. James Clarke, in his *Survey of the Lakes* (1787), makes the assertion that there had been a Benedictine monastery on Dunmallet and a nunnery on Soulby Fell, although there is no evidence for either.

from the summit was beautiful, the scenery round the lake was as rich as a fine sheet of water and woods and fruitful enclosures down to the waters edge could make it. There was formerly a roman station[53] here, and since the conquest a Benedictine nunnery[54] which once ornamented its brow, must have been an happy and picturesque conclusion to a sail down the lake. Indeed it is not a little surprizing that more of these religious houses are not to be found on these lakes, than which no place could be more suited to the idea of monkish solitude nor could the ruined tower and pointed arch, embosomed in ivy, be found in a place more beautifully calculated to inspire veneration or add a thought on other times with greater effect than here. The next morning we set out from Pooley bridge along the side of the lake for Patterdale. The road lies scarcely two hundred yards from the water, the whole of the way indeed till we got near the village of Wattermillock we never left the shore, and in Gowbarrow park the road is washed all the way by the lake on the left. We admired the situation of Mr. Robinsons house much, situated among trees and commanding a view of two reaches of the lake which here turns to the west having before spread from north west to south east. The sun shone with all its splendor when we reached the gate of Gowbarrow park, and we sat down by a little rivulet to rest ourselves, for five minutes, the cattle were cooling themselves, in the water, the lake became gently agitated, and the thick woods in the park were a fine contrast to the naked barrenness of the opposite rock. As we proceeded we saw three gentlemen whom we had before met at Grassmere, they were fishing from a boat, they acknowledged us, and informed us how far we were distant from Lyulphs tower which was then our object.[55]

In a short time we saw the turrets peeping over the trees in which they are so concealed that we had very nearly passed the building before we looked up through the trees and discovered our mistake. We knocked at the door a woman desired us to enter who showed us the inside of the tower consisting of a servants hall a long hall within used as a dining room and beyond a staircase. On the other side the door we entered, was the room belonging to the family who live there. Upstairs we had good views of the lake from the windows of the turrets. The whole is nothing more than a farm house or a gamekeepers lodge where the Duke of Norfolk to whom the park and parts of

55. Lyulph's Tower, one of Lakeland's early Gothic fantasies, was constructed as a hunting lodge by the duke of Norfolk sometime before 1783.

A watercolour of Ullswater and Lyulph's Tower by William Gell. 'Lyulphs tower looks nobly from an eminence on the water, over topped by hanging woods that terminate only by a promontory which hides the remaining part of the park from the view.'

the lake belong has two or three rooms for an occasional fishing or shooting party. The outside nearest to the lake is built of rough stones, the angles are turretted, and though from the form of the battlements and the shape of the windows, the frames of which as well as the doors are painted of a delightful pea green, the place can never be mistaken for an old building, yet at a distance where these little defects are not observed, the whole has an effect that does honour to the taste of the owner. A very civil fellow whom we took to be the gamekeeper coming in and observing us rather warm from our walk insisted on our tasting some rum and new milk which he immediately mixed and presented to us. He afterwards conducted us to Ara or Airey force, about a quarter of a mile above the house, a waterfall of about eighty feet and inferior to none that we had seen excepting the fall which exceeds all others a little distance from Buttermere.

When we had regained the road we rewarded our honest friend for his trouble and he returned his thanks and blessing. He had an openness about him in every thing he said, or did, that gained much more of our esteem than all the set speeches in the kingdom could have done, and the rusticity of his manner seemed to prove that his kindness and attention to us did not proceed from the hope of gain, but from the benevolence of his heart. There are few finer deer parks than Gowbarrow, the rocks the woods and the wildness of the place must be well adapted to the preservation of these animals and would naturally be their haunt

*Aira Force, Gowbarrow Park, Ullswater.
'He afterwards conducted us to Ara or
Airey force, about a quarter of a mile
above the house, a waterfall of about
eighty feet and inferior to none that we
had seen excepting the fall which
exceeds all others a little distance
from Buttermere.'*

if left entirely to themselves. Indeed the park is overstocked with them and we were informed that it was usual to kill as many fawns as they could catch on account of the difficulty they found in taking them at a more advanced age.

The road continued under the foliage of thick trees almost all the way to Patterdale a little past the park gate there is by far the finest view in my opinion that can be found among the lakes. On the right is a large sweep of the lake adorned with three rocky islands. Their names are House holm, Wall island and Cherry holm, behind them is a rocky and wild assemblage of hills and the beautiful village of Patterdale closes the scene. On the left are the woods of Gowbarrow and the park. Lyulphs tower looks nobly from an eminence on the water, over topped by hanging woods that terminate only by a promontory which hides the remaining part of the park from the view. Beyond this are other woods, and fields and hills in the distance, the whole is finished by the Stainmore hills in the horizon which compleat the sweetest landscape in the lakes. From this charming view we passed on to St. Patricks well,[56] which gives name to the valley, there is anually a ceremony observed here on St. Patricks day of drinking a bottle of

56. St Patrick's Well was an eighteenth-century tourist attraction; it is marked on Peter Crosthwaite's map of Ullswater. There is little to support the theory that St Patrick visited this area, and it is most likely that the name Patrick's dale, from which Patterdale is derived, was introduced by the Norse-Irish peoples in the ninth or tenth century.

Patterdale Church and Ullswater by Ackermann.

rum over the spring and on that day dancing and all sorts of merriment go on with great spirit, in honour of the tutelary Saint of this beautiful spot. We dined at the Kings Arms at the head of the lake, the people are very civil and gave us a very good dinner, after which we set out for Grassmere. We passed again by the church, in the yard is an yew tree nine yards in circumference. The way is one of the most fatiguing that can be conceived running along the side of Grisdale beck for no less than six miles of which at the least four miles and an half are up a steep fell. We were not a little pleased with the sight of Grisdale tarn, a small piece of water about three miles from Grassmere where we had been on fishing parties before. From thence the road or rather the track, lies all down hill to Grassmere and we found ourselves so thirsty from our long walk up the hill that a little well we met with would have suffered greatly from our attack if prudence had not restrained us in some measure. At this well there is a report that the old King of Patterdale once emptied an whole bottle of Rum, when on a fishing party the company were not provided with glasses. Of this Gentleman I forgot to mention that he was called king of Patterdale by hereditary right, having inherited from his ancestors an estate in the valley, upwards of two hundred pounds a year which from the remoteness of the situation is said never to have paid taxes, been disturbed by the rapacity of tyrants or plundered by the incursions of the Scots. His late majesty lived to a great age. Her majesty is yet living, and is reported to have lately given up drinking, to which she has formerly been immoderately

The Palace of Patterdale.

attached. The family name is Mounsey[57] and the present King with a fortune of eight hundred a year, which was partly scraped up by the penurious father, has the character of a gentleman of the most benevolent and charitable disposition. We arrived at Grassmere in the evening where we found another of our party waiting for our return. As he had never seen Keswick or Buttermere he crossed over the fells of Borrowdale to the latter. Two of our former party went with him. As to myself being not much attracted by the charms of Grassmere I went with my only remaining companion to Keswick intending to remain there till the return of the Buttermere party. We took a walk to friar crag, a favourite situation for viewing the Lake. Some ladies bathing at a distance, certainly more for health than pleasure for it blew a storm might have put me in mind of mermaids or Niads had not the wind been so cold as to chill every effort of the imagination and a shower of rain forced us to retreat to our inn. I this morning walked about three miles and ½ to Lowdore as I saw from friar crag it did not want water. I cannot say I was much astonished at the fall, after having seen scale force. Indeed it is no where properly speaking a fall, for there is no part of it

57. The Mounsey family enjoyed the royal title until the nineteenth century, and many of the early 'Lakers' anxiously sought a glimpse of the king or members of his household. Crosthwaite marks the 'Palace of the King of Patterdale' on his Ullswater map.

Ackermann's lithograph of Lowdore Falls. 'I this morning walked about three miles and ½ to Lowdore as I saw from friar crag it did not want water. I cannot say I was much astonished at the fall, after having seen scale force.'

*Bassenthwaite Lake by Ackermann.
'Bassenthwaite has little beauty when
compared to Derwent there is not one
island on the lake it is no where a mile
in breadth and the hills except Skiddow
are comparatively nothing.'*

where the stream falls two feet perpendicularly but the whole rushes down a bed of rocks, which are not inclined more than five and forty degrees from the horizon. I cannot think after the wonders that are related of it, that it is ever in perfection during the summer, for among other things the people say the noise can be heard at Ouse bridge at least ten miles in a direct line from the fall.

Bassenthwaite has little beauty when compared to Derwent there is not one island on the lake it is no where a mile in breadth and the hills except Skiddow are comparatively nothing. I believe the length is not much less than five miles but the scenery is unvaried and does not please after Derwent anyone whom I have heard mention it. In the evening I went up Castle crag[58] above Keswick where from the height of the rock, the whole map of Derwentwater may be perfectly discovered and eight islands plainly perceived there is a ninth not easily distinguished from this spot and Lords island looks smaller than Vicars from this point.

I endeavoured to discover any traces of the Roman fort or the Castle of the Radcliffs but though I ascended the hill with the enthusiastic eye of an antiquary I could find nothing on which to vent my conjectures or the least remnant of a foundation which from its reputed strength I could not have supposed so compleatly destroyed. The morning after I climbed Skiddow beginning my ascent from the upper end of Bassenthwaite. I cannot say I was so much pleased at the views from its summit as I expected from the accounts of others.[59] The weather was foggy when I began to ascend but before I reached the top, the sun shone out and I had an opportunity of seeing all

58. Castle Hill, not Castle Crag near Grange-in-Borrowdale. Gell's expectations of finding the remains of a Roman fort were probably increased by a passage in West's *Guide to the Lakes* which asserts that 'Castle-hill, above Keswick, is a faithful record of the existence of a station in this country. Here was the seat of the ancient lords of the manor of Derwentwater, probably raised of the ruins of the Roman fortress …'

59. Perhaps Gell had read Mrs Radcliffe's ecstatic description of the view written after an ascent of Skiddaw on horseback in 1794.

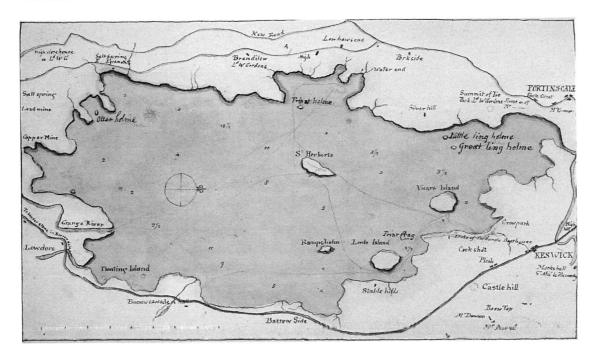

beneath me. That part of Derwentwater which I saw, looked mean from such an height and Bassenthwaite was narrow. Solway firth and the opposite shore of Scotland, on the one hand, and the Isle of Man on the other were seen indistinctly through the blue vapour in which they appeared to be enveloped. I descended by the base of Latrigg a

Gell's own map of Derwentwater and its islands. 'In the evening I went up Castle crag above Keswick where from the height of the rock, the whole map of Derwentwater may be perfectly discovered and eight islands plainly perceived …'

Gell's watercolour of Derwentwater and Skiddaw. 'I climbed Skiddow ... I cannot say I was so much pleased at the views from its summit as I expected from the accounts of others ... That part of Derwentwater which I saw, looked mean from such an height.'

smaller hill often called Skiddows' cub and gained the Penrith road about half a mile from Keswick passing over a wooden bridge raised on high rafters which joins the opposite sides of the Greeta. When I arrived at the Inn I found two of our party returned from Buttermere in company with whom I went the next morning on the lake for the second time. We touched at Lords island and compared a plan I had procured of the old house there with the ruined foundations. The island is far greater in size than Vicars, the trees flourish greatly. It is reported that when the trustees of the Grenwich hospital planted the island with young trees there were such numbers of mice on the place that the trees were soon demolished. To remedy this, numbers of cats were turned loose upon[60] the shore who lessened their number so considerably that they themselves had not enough for their subsistance. Some few were adventurous enough to tempt the waves and gained the nearest land others died on the island and some few remained long in their undisturbed retirement. Our next object was Barrow cascade the fall was really grand and the walks not ill suited to the place, a most unusual circumstance where Mr. Pocklington is concerned. We saw Lowdore again and afterwards as the wind was fair sailed for Lord William Gordons Woods intending to see his house at water end.

The situation is the most retired on the Lake, a small bay opens on the west side; and at its extremity, the house, consisting of several rooms on one floor, is overshaded by

60. Gell adds a footnote here which is strangely out of context: 'At Armathwaite Kg. Will the Conqueror founded a nunnery for black nuns with this remarkable expression "as freely as inert may it thynk or ygh may it se".' The nunnery was, in fact, founded by William Rufus, who endowed it with certain lands and possessions 'to have and to hold freely as the heart may think or eye may see'.

thick woods, while two promontories guard the north and south aspects, and Swinside shutting up the west leaves only the eastern side of the house exposed to the lake. Perhaps the view towards the lake may rather incline to the south. Along the woods are very well preserved walks which as well as the house do honour to the judgement of the owner. We sailed from thence round Trippat holme a bare and small rock to St. Herberts where we examined the plan of the hermitage if indeed it be the same which St. Herbert saw.[61] This is indeed a charming spot, when we landed the first time our haste did not permit us to walk along one of the most beautiful walks or rather avenues of firs that I ever saw. It has all the appearance of the 'Long Cathedral Isle' and being split by another row of trees near the further end, has much the effect of those Chantries or small chapels so frequent in our religious houses. The island wants but little of two furlongs in length, the breadth is not great, but the thick gloom of the wood prevents the narrowness from being observed.

We landed near the town at a little past two in the afternoon and found our appetites improved not a little by our excursion. We remained till the 23rd at Keswick when

61. Gell included plans of 'St. Herbert's Cell' and the house on Lords Island in his manuscript, and these are reproduced on page 30.

we returned to Grassmere. We had still two of our party at Buttermere whom we expected soon to join us at Grassmere. On the twenty 6th we set out for Kendal we passed through Ambleside and Clappersgate along the edge of Windermere to the ferry. Mr. Curwen has planted a border of flowering shrubs along the side of the lake for some way. I am afraid it will not have a good effect when they are large enough to be distinguished from the wild bushes which surround them. The border may be a mile or two in length, and scarcely more than ten yards in breadth so that it will have the appearance of a ribband of various colours, produced by the Liburnum the rose and other flowering shrubs.

From the Bella Grange side, is by far the better view of the islands of which there are so many as almost to divide the lake. Under the trees which overhang the ferry house we sat down to admire the view for some time. Two boats deck's in their gayest colours were just gliding gently towards the great island they had each two or three sailors on board in red jackets, and the sun shone on the whole scene in the manner that made me for the time prefer Windermere to Patterdale or Keswick. Mr. Curwen is said

62. The wheel has come full circle, as today there are too many boats on the lakes and it has been found necessary to enforce a speed limit on Windermere.

63. Kendal Castle was probably originally constructed at the close of the twelfth century, but none of the masonry now existing appears to be of earlier date than the thirteenth century. The building fell into ruin in the sixteenth century. (See *Royal Commission on Historical Monuments, Westmorland*, 1936).

to take great pleasure in his little navy. I sincerely wish Mr. Pocklington had been more attached to the amusement of sailing, than that of building, indeed the defficiency of sailing boats on the lakes can not fail to strike every observer and to a painter there must be a great and striking defect in point of picturesque beauty.[62] Windermere certainly owes much to Mr. Curwen in this respect and I believe the want of sailing vessels on the other lakes proceeds more from ignorance than the gusts and whirlwinds that come from the mountains. An island on the right hand as we crossed the ferry is called Berkshire island, and belongs to the Countess of Andover. Rawlinsons nab projects far into the water and from its crown is said to be the finest prospect of the lake.

On the left is the great island. Several vessels were anchored along the shore and they added much to the lively appearance of this beautiful and extensive lake. We arrived at Kendal about six in the evening, and saw there a miserable museum a most wretched imitation of Crosthwaites. We ascended to the castle[63] once the residence of the Lancasters Barons of Kendal one of the first families in the country and connected with the Atons Vesu Taillebois and Tysons of Alnwick. Nothing more than a small part of the shell remains. The town is neat, in the Church are monuments of the Stricklands of Sizergh; Parrs of Kendal and Bellinghams. In the morning of the 27th we set off for Milthrop passing in our way the hall at Sizergh, not long since a venerable mansion, now in conformity to the custom of the country daubed over with whitewash or plaister, so as to have lost much of its former respectable appearance. There is a tower here, built in the time of Henry the 3rd or Edward the first by William Strickland Knight, who married Elizabeth the heiress of Ralph Lord Deincourt about that time.[64] This I cannot say I particularly observed as we had not time to see the house. There are several specimens of oak carving in the house as we heard, they were executed under the direction of Walter Strickland in the time of Elizabeth or James the first. We soon after arrived at Levens, the ancient and respectable seat of the Levens family,[65] from whom this place descended to the Redman's from them to the Bellinghams and afterwards to the Graham's. An heiress of Graham brought this seat to the Suffolk family and the countess of Andover is the present possessor. We entered in front. An old hall floored with black oak

64. The pele tower at Sizergh is generally supposed to have been constructed in the latter years of the reign of Edward III (1327-1377). These solidly-built towers, which were constructed as a defence against Scottish raiders, are commonly found in the areas which border the Lake District dome, but seldom in the valleys where remoteness formed its own protection.

65. West's *Guide to the Lakes* asserts that 'Levens house was the seat of a family of that name for many ages …', but there is some confusion here. In the twelfth century the Levens Estate was owned by Ketel, third baron of Kendal, who sold one moiety of his land to the de Redeman family. The other part of the estate, now known as Nether Levens, passed into the hands of a family who bore the name of 'de Levins'.

66. Probably the *Inquisitio Eliensis*, or the Ely *Domesday* survey, referring to the counties of Cambridge, Hertfordshire, Essex, Norfolk, Huntingdon and Suffolk. In the eighteenth century, Thomas, twelfth earl of Suffolk, owned the Levens Estate. After his death in 1779, his possessions passed to his mother, Lady Andover, and, on her death, to his sister Frances.

presented itself, the wainscoat reached about two thirds of the height, above were the arms of Bellingham quartered with another coat all round the room. The ceiling was covered with plaister mouldings, over the chimney place hung two or three frames containing the genealogy of the family, in another frame I observed the copy of the Ely[66] roll which was drawn in the time of the conqueror. Under the staircase is a place used as a chapel, above are many lodging rooms. In one is an handsome state bed at least it has formerly been so. From the hall a few steps on the left hand conduct you to an handsome apartment, in the windows of which the arms of the Bellinghams and their matches are painted. In this room are some of the oak carvings, mentioned by West, as placed here by James Bellingham to imitate the taste of his neighbour Walter Strickland of Sizergh, but if the carvings at Sizergh, be neither superior, or in greater profusion than here, this is only another instance of the fallacy of Mr. Wests eyesight, who must have possessed a peculiar faculty of magnifying and multiplying whatever came in his way. The river Kent runs through the park where it falls near twenty feet. There is much fine timber on the estate and nothing is

spoiled by any modern alteration, except the house which is whitewashed all over on the outside. The garden preserves the same form as it recieved from a gardner of King James the firsts, who says West, 'resided here with colonel

Levens Hall and gardens. 'Its peculiarity consists in clipped yew trees or cypresses, which distinguish the terraces and gardens of that time ...'

67. Monsieur Beaumont was James II's gardener. After the 'Glorious Revolution', he came to Levens Hall where he was employed by Colonel James Graham, a Jacobite sympathiser. The topiary gardens have changed little since they were laid out in the seventeenth century.

68. Milnthorpe, Westmorland, then a small port on the River Bela.

69. Probably limestone pavement produced by the chemical weathering of Carboniferous Limestone.

Graham during part of the troubles of his royal master,[67] Its peculiarity consists in clipped yew trees or cypresses, which distinguish the terraces and gardens of that time, it is laid out in small formal beds bordered with box; the walks are of turf. We dined at Millthrop[68] seven miles from Kendal and after dinner went to enquire for the captain of a vessel to whom we had been recommended by a Gentleman of Kendal. We found him at work in his hay field and he informed us he meant to sail on the 29th for Liverpool. We returned to Millthrop to procure provisions, and settle with our Landlady there, and the next morning returned to Mr. Cartwright our captain at whose house we remained till our embarcation. A very short distance from the house upon the hill that rises gently from the sands is one of the most curious rocks I ever saw and indeed perhaps the only one of the kind. A large flat surface of rock about an hundred yards each way is intersected with cracks and fissures some of which are three or four yards deep exactly in the stile of clay where after having been wet it is dried by the heat of the sun.[69] Some little puddles of clay which we found on the rock gave us an opportunity of observing how exactly similar the cracks were in each, the only difference was in size, and softness for the colour is exactly the same. I believe the fuellists and antifuellists as they are called or in other words, those who refer to the influence of fire, the present appearance of the earth and those who ascribe everything to the universal deluge would find here reason to assent in some degree to the opinions of each other. We slept at our captains house and were as much pleased with the treatment we experienced, as we were with the modesty of their charge, which was only five shillings for two nights and a day between us both. Two of our companions were gone to a small village nearer to the vessel. We went on board about half past ten, after having walked six miles over the wet sand and waded through two rivers, one of which was very rapid.[70] At about half past four we weighed anchor but we had not been under sail ten minutes before we had the misfortune to hear that we were on a sand bank, and must remain there till about half past two in the next morning in the same situation.

We set sail on the return of the tide, the wind was not in our favour, yet not so much against us, as to oblige us to tack, about five in the morning we saw Peel Castle, to the right, and the isle of Walney a low flat island, about nine

70. The vessel was carrying gunpowder from Milnthorpe to Liverpool, and it appears that, after she was loaded, she stood off in the estuary as a safety precaution. This would explain the long walk across the sands in order to board the ship.

71. Arnside Tower was built as a pele tower probably in the fifteenth century. It was destroyed in 1602, but repaired and inhabited until the later part of the seventeenth century.

72. Gell is unsure of the name of this tower and records the word 'Haslop,' but it seems likely that the tower which could be seen from the ship was Hazelslack Tower, another pele, built in the fourteenth century.

73. Dallam Tower, formerly a pele, but rebuilt by Daniel Wilson in 1720-22.

74. Gunpowder was manufactured at several places in southern Cumbria at this time, and was in part a product of the charcoal industry which flourished in this area. West's *Guide to the Lakes* (2nd edition, 1780) notes that in the vicinity of Sedgwick, south of Kendal, 'large works for the manufactory of gunpowder have been lately erected'.

miles in length and not one in breadth. On the left were the two towers of Arnside,[71] and Haslop[72] which as the vulgar believe were built by some great man, together with Dalham tower[73] for the residence of his three daughters and coheirs. The two first in ruins the last inhabited, and entirely rebuilt by a gentleman of the name of Wilson who resides at the tower, within quarter of a mile from Millthrop. Not long after we saw Lancaster and a miserable flat coast which stretches from thence to Liverpool on which is situated Blackpool, a place of late much frequented by the inhabitants of both towns, as a summer residence. There is not a single tree near it nor indeed could I percieve one the whole voyage. About half past two we began to app-roach Liverpool and the tide favouring us we soon arrived at the powder magazine, after we had passed the beacon. Here we left our vessel as the Captain was obliged to unload about twelve tons of Gunpowder[74] which had been conveyed through a most terrible storm of thunder and lightening all the way from Millthrop. The boat landed us at the docks about three miles higher up and on the other side of the river. We slept at Liverpool and in the morning after seeing as much of the town as our time would permit took a passage in the Chester packet for Eastham about seven miles from the Mersey. The morning was fine a brisk wind sprung up and in about three quarters of an hour we reached the spot where we were to meet the coach which conveyed us to Chester.

Acknowledgements

My sincere thanks go to Barrow Public Library for their permission to publish this manuscript, the copyright of which remains vested in Cumbria Heritage Services. I also wish to thank Mr Ron Sands of the reference section of Barrow Library, Mr M R Bruce, Lt Col John Chandos-Pole and Christine Denmead.

Two other main sources have been used to supplement Gell's watercolours and sketches: *The Lake District*, published in 1821 by R Ackermann; and a volume of engravings by Joseph Farington published in 1789.

The portrait of William Gell is reproduced by courtesy of the National Portrait Gallery, London; and *Buttermere* by J M W Turner by courtesy of the Tate Gallery, London.

Additional illustrations are taken from the editor's own collection.

William Rollinson,
Ulverston, 2000

Publisher's note: the final stages of proofreading and indexing were undertaken by Christine Denmead and Paul Hindle.

Index of Places

Modern spellings are used. Illustrations are shown in *italic*.

William Rollinson:
An Afterword by Melvyn Bragg

William Rollinson, who died during the preparation of this book on the 22nd March 2000 aged sixty-two, was the leading historical geographer of the Lake District — probably the best there has ever been. He published a number of books, one of which, *The Lake District — Life And Traditions*, is a classic which will endure as long as anyone is interested in Wordsworth's patch of ground. He was an outstanding lecturer with a substantial personal following in the North-West. In an area carefully combed and commented on over 250 years, he made an original and substantial contribution. He spread the word on local radio and Border Television, never lowering his standards.

Bill Rollinson was born in Barrow-in-Furness on the 2nd August 1937. His father was a bricklayer at the Barrow iron and steel works. After Barrow Grammar School for Boys, he took a first in geography at Manchester University. In 1962, he became a lecturer at Liverpool University, eventually moving to the Department of Continuing

William Rollinson,
1937–2000.

Education, from where he retired in his late fifties. He continued to lecture to local societies in the far North-West, increased his published output and found a niche in local broadcasting.

Bill's first public work was an article on the 'Lost Villages and Hamlets of Low Furness'. His last, a trio of booklets, *Making Charcoal*, *Making Drystone Walls* and *Making Swill Baskets*. Between those typically local and particular concerns came several outstanding works on the landscape, traditions and language of Cumbria. These were what fascinated him, particularly the Scandinavian connection.

Although he was, in a very competitive field, supreme in his work on the Lake District, there was perhaps an even deeper pull to Norway, especially to the Fjord Mundal. Probably his best television documentary, and most charming book, compares Mundal and Wastwater — uncannily similar in look and history. Bill was entranced by the connections and, year after year; hauled boatloads and busloads of hardy audiences to Iceland and Norway to examine the origin of the folk who, more than a millennium ago, became the core settlers in the Lakes, giving it its unique language and character.

I first met Bill more than thirty years ago, when he came to see me at the small, half-derelict cottage in north Cumbria in which I was hoping to live. I was hopelessly digging out some obstinate raspberry canes. Bill rolled up his sleeves — literally — gave me a hand, stayed for tea, then for supper, and from then on he became a closer and closer friend of the family.

He was an old-fashioned unreconstructed bachelor. Doctor Watson would have recognised a fellow spirit. My family, especially our children, welcomed his kindly, adult, wise presence, and were as shaken as I was when they learned that an early death was inevitable.

I worked with Bill on several television and radio programmes, most ambitiously a series of six one-hour documentaries on the history of the Border Television area — the Lakes, the Borders themselves and the Isle of Man. He was determined that images — of which he had a robust distrust — should not eclipse content, and his incisive interference was often a pain in the neck, but one which the whole crew genuinely appreciated because we knew he was aiming for something that mattered. The result, I think, was a series that is both authoritative and lively on a subject that lends itself too easily to scenery, lush music and undemanding thought.

When you walked with Bill along, say, Buttermere to Haystacks, you walked through millions of years of geology, centuries of history and, above all, a landscape of language. He had a deep pleasure uncoupling words and showing where they came from — usually from Norse; if this sounds boring, believe me, it was gripping. Sometimes, when he chatted on as we concentrated on getting up something steep, it encroached a little too much, but even that was memorable.

Bill was a man who gave. He never came to see us without bringing gifts of some sort, but when you gave back to him, he was abashed. Although he was as welcome as spring, he had to be importuned to stay overnight, even after thirty years. This was shyness, perhaps a deeper loneliness at the heart of a man abundantly endowed with friends and always true to his Barrovian working-class roots. His politics were Labour, his characteristics were North British, yet he enjoyed meeting the great and influential in the county as he did in the course of his comprehensive scaling of the Lakes.

It is difficult to see Bill Rollinson being replaced — that devotion, that scholarship, that happy 'narrow cell'. Whenever I thought of the Lakes, I thought of Bill, and that will not change. His ashes are scattered on Westmorland Cairn, Great Gable.

Reprinted by kind permission of the *Guardian*.